DEDICATION

To my spouse, Rufus Roberts.

To my children Spencer, Preston, Brittney, and Joshua Roberts.

To my family not just my blood family but
the one I married into too.

To my friends who daily deposit something positive in my life.

To my church family – Elizabeth Holiness Church and
the Pastor, Bishop Anderson Williams.

To the church of COOLJC and the
Apostle Walter Lee Jackson, Region 8.

To the Catholic church where I was raised and went to school.

To my grandparents, Franklin and Isabell Jenkins who
raise me to give reverence to God.

To my parents Albert and France Smith.

To Colleton County Department of Social Services
where I worked 33 years.

The 4 C's of a Successful Testimony:

THE TESTIMONY of RUBINA ROBERTS

RUBINA ROBERTS

MARTINA
PUBLISHING
INC.
Walterboro, SC

Special Thanks to:
Shiela M. Keaise, who served as the editor and consultant for this book.

The 4 C's of a Successful Testimony.
Copyright © 2017 by Rubina Roberts. All rights reserved. No part of this book may be reproduced in any written, electronic, recording, or photocopying form without written permission of the author.

Martina Publishing, Inc.
PO Box 1216, Walterboro, SC 29488
www.ShielaMartina.com

The 4 C's of a Successful Testimony/Rubina Roberts. Summary: This book gives examples of how anyone can have a successful testimony if she gives Jesus her life, puts others ahead, and follows the example of Jesus.

Library of Congress Control Number: 2017908609

Scripture quotations from:
The Holy Bible, King James Version. ©2015 All Rights Reserved

ISBN: 978-0-9799344-5-2
[1. Testimony-Nonfiction. 2. Godly living-Nonfiction. 3. King James Version-Bible. 4. Christianity-Lifestyle. 1. Title

Words italicized are my direct quotes, paraphrases and testimony.

10 9 8 7 6 5 4 3 2 1
Printed in the United States of America

CONTENTS

6
PREFACE

9
INTRODUCTION

12
CHAPTER ONE: CONFESS

21
CHAPTER TWO: CLAIM

27
CHAPTER THREE: CHOOSE

36
CHAPTER FOUR: CREATE

43
CHAPTER FIVE: WHAT IS YOUR TESTIMONY?

49
ABOUT THE AUTHOR

PREFACE

Once you read this book, your life will never be the same again. If you accept what the Holy Spirit leads me to tell you, and apply them to your life, you will see change. I am just a simple person with no special title. I am someone who loves the Lord and realizes that Jesus' love is enough for me. I do not let people tell me who I am. I am a witness that God can use simple people to do extraordinary things. Nobody is better than you. You just have to trust God. If we fall in love with God and do not let anything separate us from His love, we can be used by God to do the impossible.

I know that I had a call to share my testimony, but this does not mean that I am trying to preach. Being a preacher has always been the farthest thing from my mind. God did not call everyone to preach, but he did call all of us to tell our testimony. This means that we should tell others how God has brought us out; not for self-glory but to help someone else grow in the Lord. If this is your goal, God will put your life on the right course so no man can hinder you.

The Lord has already told us to seek first the kingdom of God and all these things shall be added unto us. So just be happy just the way your heavenly father has made you. Ask your heavenly father to complete the good work he has already started in you. The Lord has a plan for your life and knows the journey you have to take and will go through. Never be satisfied when you reach one goal; set another one.

The closer I got to finishing this book, the harder the devil fought me. The Lord had already made a way of escape for me, because He knew that this book would be a blessing to those who would read it. And it is meant to be a blessing to share and encourage you!

Here are two reasons why I wanted to share my testimony and why you should share yours:

1. **I want to share the good things God has done for me, because the Bible tells me to.**
    a) Psalm 71:15-16 I will declare your righteousness and your salvation every day, though I do not fully understand what the outcome will be. Lord God, I will come in the power of your mighty acts, remembering your righteousness—yours alone.
    b) Mark 5:19 But Jesus said, "No, go home to your family, and tell them everything the Lord has done for you and how merciful he has been."
    c) Psalm 22:22 I will praise you to all my brothers; I will stand up before the congregation and testify of the wonderful things you have done.
    d) Psalm 66:16 Come and listen, all you who fear God, and I will tell you what he did for me.
    e) John 15:26-27 "When the Helper comes, whom I will send to you from the Father—the Spirit of Truth, who comes from the Father—he will testify on my behalf. You will testify also, because you have been with me from the beginning."
    f) 1 John 1:2-3 This life was revealed to us, and we have seen it and testify about it. We declare to you this eternal life that was with the Father and was revealed to us. What we have

seen and heard we declare to you so that you, too, can have fellowship with us. Now this fellowship of ours is with the Father and with his Son, Jesus, the Messiah.

g) Psalm 35:28 My tongue will declare your righteousness and praise you all day long.

h) Daniel 4:2 "I want you all to know about the miraculous signs and wonders the Most High God has performed for me."

2. **I want to encourage others.**
   a) 1 Thessalonians 5:11 Wherefore comfort yourselves together, and edify one another, even as also ye do.
   b) Hebrews 10:24-25 And let us continue to consider how to motivate one another to love and good deeds, not neglecting to meet together, as is the habit of some, but encouraging one another even more as you see the day of the Lord coming nearer.
   c) 1 Thessalonians 5:14 We urge you, brothers, to admonish those who are idle, cheer up those who are discouraged, and help those who are weak. Be patient with everyone.

- Rubina Roberts

INTRODUCTION

God has a plan for our lives. He wants us to seek to be a blessing to others for that's when blessings will follow us. Everyone can encourage someone when they are going through by simply saying, "You can make it." What you give to someone will come back to you. The Bible reminds us, "…What you measure will be measured back to you." My grandmother always told me to treat people well, because you will reap what you sow. Even when they don't treat you good, let the Lord handle it. The Lord has already told us that revenge is His.

When you see someone with a hindrance spirit trying to stop your blessing, pray for them and ask God to help them. But it is still up to that person to want to be changed. They may never change, but you did your part. When you go around trying to be a blessing to others, no one can stop your blessing. If you make a mistake, learn from it and use it to help someone else. Life is like a Checkers game. You have to check with God to make sure you make the right moves in life. Thus, when you allow God to take control, you will be the winner. Just like you hear "King me" in checkers, you will hear God say "Well done." You can stand when the wind blows, because you know you checked with God.

Like any game, you have to ask the Lord to help you play fairly. I have learned that if I want to please God, I can't please people.

The Bible says to "owe no man anything but love." To enjoy your life you have to know that God loves you and that you are important to him. Do not let anybody be the source of your happiness but God—not work, children, husband, friends, nor material things. We are all on the same playing field, just one prayer away from being blessed or one decision away from not being blessed.

Some of the decisions I made that caused me not to be blessed were…

1. Allowing people's negative words to lower my self-esteem.
2. Letting past hurt hinder my future.
3. Taking revenge in my own hand.
4. Not forgiving others when they wronged me.
5. Putting my trust in people and not God.
6. Finding fault in people instead of praying for them.

Don't worry how strong the winds may blow, just trust God. Some days are harder than others, but as long as you keep on trusting in God, he will make your latter days greater than your beginning.

The prayers that I confessed that caused me to be blessed are:

1. God I will love myself with your help.
2. God I will accept your love to be sufficient for me.
3. God I will be mindful to always be a blessing to others.
4. God I will always pay my tithes as you give me increase.
5. God I will seek to please you instead of man.

The things God will bless us with are only a part of our happiness. Jesus is the true source of our peace, joy, and happiness. In this book which is my testimony, I would like to share how you too can have a happy and successful relationship with God and man by making the 4 C's a part of your testimony:

1. **Confess** your sins, what you want God to do, and that you are helpless without God;
2. **Claim** your life as a follower of Jesus and that you will live for Him;
3. **Choose** to stay focused on God's purpose for your life, to forgive others and to be obedient to God;
4. **Create** your destiny by trusting God to fight your battles.

CHAPTER ONE

Confess

It is so important to confess your sins and let God know that you are a sinner and need to be saved. Do not let people take your joy with their hateful, mean, evil spirit. Ask God to lead you in the right direction. Do not lean on your own understanding. Confess that the joy of the Lord is your strength. The Lord has already told us that he will perfect those things that concerns us. The Bible tells us to seek first the kingdom of God and all these things shall be added to us. God requires that we do our best to live righteously. Ask God to help and show you what you need to learn from what you just went through to make your life better.

Once God saves you, don't let the enemy steal your joy. Keep the joy of the Lord and you will always have a good, loving, kind spirit. The joy of the Lord is your strength. Everyone, even your enemies, should not come in contact with you and be the same. They should leave out of your presence better than they came. If you do things that you enjoy as unto the Lord, you will benefit from them. Enjoy your life!

Confess that you will love yourself. One important thing to do is that you love yourself. You don't need people to tell you that you are important. Rather, you know that you love yourself when people say unkind words and you don't let it affect you. You must pray and ask God to make you the best person that he wants you to become. In order to live a great life, you have to be courageous, bold, and obedient to the will of God. Out of jealousy, people will try to control you and make you do what they want you to do. They will let anything come out of their mouths to make you feel bad.

I thank the Lord for giving me the opportunity to be His servant. I don't know what tomorrow holds, but I do know if I keep on trusting God, it will turn out good. I know that God has a plan that is great for my life. All I have to do is walk by faith to the end.

Confess that you need God and that you are helpless without Him. By acknowledging the Lord in all your ways, he shall direct your path. God and only God should be the one directing your path. You cannot let people direct your path, because you will never end up to a perfect end. When you let the Lord direct your path, you might have some struggles, but your end result will be great. You have to believe that prayer can change anything around. In everyone's life, some failure does occur, but continue to trust God and he will give you double for your trouble.

Every time I go through something, I confess that I will not be the same. Even when people start talking about me, I keep my mind on God. I tell the Lord that revenge is His and I will not take the time to fight.

The Bible says that some things come through fasting and praying.

You should learn how to fast and pray more to stay positive and focused. It is your responsibility not to let people hinder you from being happy. You need to learn that no weapon formed against you will prosper. All things will work together for your good if you love the Lord and are called by Him. People will speak well of you as long as you are doing everything they want you to do. Once you stop pleasing people and start doing what God wants you to do, their talk will change. Who wants to be a puppet for people?

Just like the Holy Spirit let me know, He will let you know. If a sister or brother is mad with another person, there is no reason for you to get mad with "that person" just because a sister or brother is mad with "that person." That would be just like the devil. Wild animals, in most occasions, will not attack unless they feel afraid of you. God told us to love our enemies.

I had to quote scriptures on the devil and plead the blood of Jesus when fear comes upon me. When I plead the blood of Jesus over and over in my mind or out loud, the devil does not attack that area in my life.

If you want the Holy Ghost to keep the devil from attacking your life and mind, you can speak out loud whatever you have to get victory over in your mind. It will be a fight at times, but it will be worth it. I am not saying you will not have to shed some tears, but if you ask God to help you learn from that situation, your life will never be the same again. Jesus did not just die on Calvary for you to have second best. He bleed and died for you to have the very best life possible.

Know what battles to fight. If you turn your battles over to God, you will become happier then you could ever dreamed. He told us to acknowledge Him in all our ways and He will direct our paths. When God gets ready to move on your behalf, obstacles always come. Just ask God what He wants you to do in that situation. You may find out that He may just want you to stand still and leave the fighting to him.

After confessing it, take some action to improve your life. Ask God if you need to continue friendships with any persons that make you feel miserable. You should not let anyone make you feel less than. Stop talking about how you are going to improve your life. Sometimes all we do is talk and never put anything into action. We say what we are going to do, but we don't let God help us to do it.

If you want to improve your life, you must have faith in God and believe what the Bible says. "Faith without works are dead." You have to ask God to help you stay focused on what He wants you to do; not just talk about it. If you want to hear the Lord and Savior say, "Well done my good and faithful servant," you have to confess your sins and run this race with faith.

When we are going through, God wants to see if we will rest in, trust in, and have faith in him. Fear may arise, but we do not have to let fear get the best of us. If we don't let obstacles stop us along the way but trust in God, the Lord will make us perfect as He is perfect. The Lord told us that blessings are going to overtake them who overcome. When we go through our test the right way, God blesses us beyond what we could ever dream. These blessings are given by God to His glory when we go through. It is for the glory of God when the enemy fights you and you can still give praise to God. Once you give God His glory, He will give you your glory. When that glory comes upon you, don't let anyone stop you from enjoying God's blessing. People may wonder about your story, but they do not know what you had to go through to get that glory.

When I was going through, I had to trust God to go with me to a special meeting and to take away fear from what people would say; I had to walk in faith. I regrouped and started quoting scriptures. As I trusted the Holy Spirit's guidance and walked in faith, God walked with me. The meeting went very well. Instead of me being afraid of what the people would say, the Lord told me what to say. The Holy Spirit caused me to impress without making a mess. I walked in faith and God provided for me that very hour. The older I get, the more I learn that I can't depend on anyone to make me happy but God.

So it is your responsibility to make yourself happy. Do not give anybody that much power that you say, "I am not happy because of you." The Lord told us the affliction of the righteous are many but he will deliver us from them all. Life can be like a roller coaster, up and down, and all kinds of crazy twists. As you trust God and let Him direct your path, you will always have a perfect ending. No pain, no growth. If you have no pain you will have no growth. We don't like pain but pain helps us to grow. Out of pain and waiting on God comes a more anointed life, because you have to trust God, pray and fast.

God will show you who really has your best interest at heart. Let God show you who does not have your best interest at heart.

People will smile in your face and mean you no good. They get what they can from you and give nothing in return. When God blesses, you should bless someone else. I learned that the more I encourage others, the more God blesses me. If you be obedient to what God Is telling you to do, trouble won't last as long. Seek to be in the will of God so you can stay blessed. God wants to be in the plan for your life. If God is not in your plans, invite him in to clean it up and make it better for you.

The Bible tells us that we will give an account for every idol word that comes out of our mouths. Do not go through life trying to hurt people or making their life miserable. Saying and doing hurtful and evil things to people on the job just to get ahead will only make your life miserable. Make sure your conscious is clear. Do not let anyone cause you not to enjoy your life.

Be careful what you speak over your children. Even when you see a negative behavior, you have to speak a positive word over their life. No matter how bad a child may be, he or she does not want to always hear, "You are the bad one." Your child would like to hear "You need to act like Jesus's child." When you do, God will reward you with good. Positive words and love will turn around anybody. If a child hears his parent say, "You're bad and you are just like your daddy or mother", the child will continue to act like him or her. It is better if that child hears a parent talking and praying to God. She learns that through faith nothing is impossible when you trust God and ask God to help you to do better.

You have to watch your attitude. If you are mad at life and yell and scream at your children for no reason, you display a negative attitude. When you are on stressful job, don't bring that stress to your family. You are literally destroying your family. When you had a bad day, don't take it out on the children. Teach your children to trust in Jesus by how you handle every situation. The best investment you can make for your children is to show them how to live for God so they can enjoy their childhood. Allow your children to watch TV, but make sure you read the Bible with them too. Yelling and screaming at your spouse is not a good example for your children. As you learned how to be a servant to your children, spouse, and people you come in contact with, you show by example how to live Godly. Do not let wrong words cause our children and spouse not to blossom where they are.

Even when people hurt you, use positive words to turn it around. Give the Lord any battles you have to fight. Do not fight them on your own nor use negative words. Remember you will give an account for every idle word you speak. Instead of using negative words, use positive words to say what you need to say. Every time you hurt someone, you will feel that same hurt one way or another. So be careful what words you use.

One small word or action could cause a wild fire. If you cause a wild fire, be willing to say, "I am sorry." When someone is talking about someone, do not respond negatively. Instead, say, "We need to pray for them." Do not respond negatively at all or talk about anyone when they make a bad decision. Instead choose a small act of kindness or a big act of thoughtfulness to turn around a wild fire. Whatever you do, make it your business not to cause one. You do not want to stop God's blessing out of your life.

When I started being careful about my words and my actions, my family members improved. I don't know why but when I became stressed, depressed, and mad with someone else, I would take it out on my family members. Then I expected God to answer my prayers concerning them; He didn't. My trouble lasted a whole lot longer. However, when I started being careful not to use negative words and stopped hurtful actions, things started to change. Not to say that problems didn't come, but things worked out a whole lot faster. God turned the problem around for my good. Every problem that I faced when I am doing my best to live right, God used them to make me perfect.

You have to be careful about your words and actions around your children. They follow exactly what you do and mock what you say. If you get mad for no reason and start yelling and screaming at them, they will yell and scream when something they don't like happens to them. Some of our children's bad behavior are picked up from us. When you curse at your children, or they hear you curse, you are teaching them that cursing is okay. We need to communicate with our children the right way so that they will know how to communicate the right way.

My Testimony

Like the Hebrew boys, you will see the fire and smell the fire, but rest assure God will bring you out without one hair singed. I'm a witness that if you trust in God, you will not only endure in the mist of the fire, you will not fear what men can do to you. If you let it, fear will cause you to miss out on what God has for you. That is why it's so important to seek God for your next move. The wrong move will cause you to miss out on what God has for you. Do as I have done… Confess that you are the righteousness of God.

The greater the struggle the better the blessing. One of the lessons I learned in a testimony concerning my son, God told me, "In this battle you don't have to fight." After my son was falsely accused and arrested, God spoke to me and told me to let Him fight for my child. All He required of me was obedience to His commands. My son was put in jail and while there, he picked up the Bible and God lead him to read Exodus 15:22-23, which talks about the Israelites traveling in the wilderness and the food running out. God provided water and food for them while they were in the wilderness. My son told me that the Lord spoke to him from that passage and told him that if he walked up rightly before him, God would provide him with food, shelter, and even a cell phone. I thought to myself, "My child is totally off track. God is not concerned about cell phones." Then, the Holy Spirit spoke to me about what my son said and I believed my son was telling me the truth. The Spirit said that this generation has made cell phones a need and if they walk upright before God he would provide all their needs, even a cell phone. Not long after, my son was acquitted of all the charges and he has an upgraded cell phone. Not only is he doing well, he is spreading the gospel to his peers about how God will provide your needs. AMEN!

CHAPTER TWO

Claim

You have to claim victory in your life by acknowledging Jesus as your Savior. When the wind blows you cannot let that stop you from living for God. To get the best from God you have to claim what God has purposed for your life. You cannot let anything stop you from reaching for the stars. I learned that the greater the struggle the better the blessing. When the enemy comes in like a flood, draw close to God and hear what he has to say about what you need to do in that situation. He wants you to know that in this battle that every great struggle are just lining you up for your next blessing.

When life knocks you down, you have to get back in the fight. Do not take too long feeling sorry for yourself. The Word of God told you that everything works together for your good. When you find a hindrance in your life, you have to move it as soon as possible. It will cause you to go around in circles and will not take you to a better place. Similarly, struggles will hinder your growth. Some of you can move quicker than others from these hindrances. The best way to deal with hindrances is to be patient and seek the face of God so that it does not affect you negatively. You have to let the devil know that if anyone has a nervous breakdown, it is going to be him. The devil will see that what he is trying to use to destroy you is giving you a closer walk with God. Every time a situation arises, use scripture and he will leave you alone. Too much gossiping and worrying about someone can hinder you and cause you to go in circles. The Lord wants us to pray and not gossip about what someone else is doing. Claim your life as a follower of Jesus and live for Him.

You have to be determined every time you make a mistake to turn the page and start all over again. You have to be more focused on your future than you are on the things around you that hinder you. You can't let the world tell you who you are. You have to know that the greater one lives inside of you. God has a purpose for your life. You have to be determined that your past hurt and disappointments will not mess up your future. When you get a bad attitude and keep a negative outlook, they will mess up your future. So keep a positive attitude and let God write a new and better story for you.

The more pain and hurt you go through can help encourage someone else to become a better person. The more you help someone else, the more God will bless you. If you make a mistake and learn from it, you can help to make your life better and help someone else. Ask the Lord to teach you what he wants you to learn from your mistakes. As things get hard, be determine to put one foot in front of the other and keep on walking and believing. You will learn what you need to learn out of the situation. Just walk in perfect love, don't hold any unforgiveness in your heart, and keep the joy of the Lord — anticipating that God will bless you. And He will.

Psalm 30:15 says, "Weeping may endure for a night but joy cometh in the morning." I don't know what morning you will wake up with joy, but I do know that it is going to come. This is why every day when you wake up, you should be determined not to let anyone stop your joy. How much better it is for God to bless you when you have a positive attitude and forgiving heart. Claim your life as a follower of Jesus and live for Him.

You have to wake up with your mind on God (despite what others may do or already has done to you. When you wake up, God should be the first person you talk to. Ask Him to help you keep a positive attitude so someone will be blessed. The quickest way for God to bless you is when you pray for someone else. Try it every day and walk upright before God. Some days you fall short, but get right back up again. Keep trying your best. Ask God to help you to do better. Nobody knows your heart but God and no one can bless you like God. Man can give you a lot of things, but no one can give you peace but God. Without peace there is no happiness. All you have to do to get peace is ask God and be obedient to His Word. The Word told us in Psalm 84:11 that "no good thing will he withhold from them that walk uprightly."

Be courageous enough to rise above your enemy. Do not hold anything against them. Psalm 110:1 tells us "…until I make your enemies a footstool for your feet." That's why it is important that you let God fight your battle. Because when you fight, you miss out on the promise of God. Romans 12:19 says, "Vengeance is mine; I will repay," saith the Lord. We want the benefits without being obedient to the Word of God. It does not work that way. You are going to have to leave revenge in the hand of God in order to be happy and free. This is how you rise above your enemy. You have to be determined to make your life better. This is how you can keep peace in your life in every bad situation. Do you know how to find the silver lining in every circumstance? Be careful what comes out of your mouth. Make sure you are thankful to God for everything you are given, and let the things you do and say benefit those around you.

It is also important that you do not show favoritism. None of your children should feel that one child is favored over another. This can only lower your child's self-esteem. That's why it is so important to watch the words you say to your children. You don't want your words to destroy your child or anyone else. Matthew 12:36 says, "But I say unto you, that every idle word that men shall speak, they shall give account thereof in the day of judgment." Claim your life as a follower of Jesus and live for Him.

Be determine to give God His glory even if it makes you uncomfortable for a while. He will show you His glory when you learn how to handle it the way the Bible says. We get no glory when we handle things our way—only misery. As we decide to handle it God's way, God gets the glory. Then and only then will He turn our mourning into dancing. The more God blesses you, the more He wants you to bless someone else. What you make happen for someone else, God will make happen for you. As long as you keep sowing good seeds, you are going to reap a good harvest.

When God saves us, we should always want to pull some one out of the fire. If you want to do something in life to better yourself, simply pray about it first and put your whole heart into it. Once you give it your best shot, do not worry about what people think about you or even if things don't go the way you want them to go. If you put God first in everything, it will turn out better than you would ever dreamed. The key is to pray and put God first in everything you do.

My Testimony

The harder the enemy fights you, the more you should trust God and the stronger you will become. The Bible also tells us, "Many are the afflictions of the righteous, but God delivers us from them all." I have learned that everything you go through, if you don't let it make you bitter, it will make you better. Let your tests and trials make your life better. Do as I have done… Claim the victory over your problems, your enemies, and your bad situations.

My husband and I prayed and asked the Lord to show us what He wanted us to learn from our son's experience. During our son's dilemma, we did not have to pay for a lawyer or do anything except wait on God. We prayed and trusted God to work out our son's problem. And He did! During this time, the Lord touched my husband's heart and he accepted his call to ministry. After being a deacon for at least ten years, my husband felt God leading him to become an Elder in the church. His trial sermon was, "This Is Just a Test." Now, my husband prays and fasts more, reads his Bible more, and reaches more people to encourage them to hold on despite what they go through. What the enemy meant for harm with our son's bad experience, God turn it around for our good - My husband accepted a higher call for his life. Praise the Lord. AMEN!

CHAPTER THREE

Choose

We must choose to stay focused on the will of God. This means that we must not put our minds on things other than God's purpose for our lives. When you stay focused, everything starts to line up because you are acknowledging God as you go. Not only are you happier, every problem that arises, God will take care of it. When we stay focused on what God has for us to do, we can speak to the enemy and tell him that God said He will make perfect that which concerns me. Ask the Lord to help you deal with hindrances that lead you around in circles. You may get tired, but the Bible says, "Let the weak say I am strong."

You have to make a decision that your feelings are not going to get the best of you. The closer you get to the finish line, the harder it may seem to get. You have to know what battles to fight. You can't fight every battle. You have to stay focused in order to finish. When things get too hard, stay focused. When things are not going good and cause you to mess up, just stay focused on God's will for your life.

God promises to work things out when we stay focused and trust God. Our children need us to stay focused. Most of the time our children suffer during their childhood, because we don't stay focused. When we don't, we miss good fellowship with our children while they are growing. We may miss some of the experiences that may change their lives forever. This will happen, because we didn't put our trust in God and stay focused. Don't worry how hard the enemy fights you. Instead of fighting back, do what is right for God and let God fight for you.

Stay focused on your happiness and your peace in God. He will bless you with a healthy long life. If you lack staying focused, ask the Lord to help you get back focused on the things of Him. Sometimes you get off track and you don't even know that you've gotten off track. The things in life you think you need to make you happy may be the very things that will make you miserable. Only the Lord knows what will make you happy. Put first things first by asking the Lord to help you put Him first. Ask him to help you be a better wife, a better mother, and a better person. Try to be a blessing to others.

Stay focused on what is ahead. God can't bless you beyond what you can't believe him to do. He has already told you that "eyes have not seen nor ears have not heard nor has entered into the heart of man what he has for you."

Stay focused on the purpose and not the people. Don't let unhappy people make your life miserable. People will try to make themselves look good and try to make you look bad. Just ignore them and ask the Lord to help you in the areas you fall short. Do not stop! Keep fighting the good fight of faith. All other battles, let the Lord do your fighting. Do not worry about what people think about you. Worry more about what God thinks about you.

My one goal is to totally please God and not man. My future is in God's hand and not man's hand. Romans 8:31 says, "What shall we say to these things? If God be for us who can be against us." When I stay focused, I don't make any major decision in my life without praying and fasting just to make sure God is in the plan. Then I will know that this is the next move God has for me. I have learned never to lean on my own understanding, no matter how sure I am.

When other people make decisions that are going to affect you, make sure you pray and fast before you follow them. Married women, your husband is the head of the house and when he is getting ready to make a decision, you need to pray that his decision does not affect the family negatively. Nobody wants to be treated like a child, but it is a good idea to pray about every decision we make and get God's permission before you act.

While it is important to let the people around us enjoy their lives, we should pray for them so they won't make some unnecessary mistakes. The more you bless someone else, the more God will bless you. We should bless others with our prayers. So stay focused and don't stop living Godly because everything is not going your way or if people are talking about you. Live on purpose and with the help of the Lord you will enjoy life even the more. When you are living a life of purpose with faith, God will little by little change your life to help others. You cannot wait for someone else to do it. Ask the Lord to help you do it. Speak the best for yourself and family and watch God do it for you.

The most important thing in your life is to forgive. We have to choose to forgive the way God forgives us. Jesus prayed, "…forgive us our trespasses as we forgive those who trespass against us." We have to make a decision to forgive and not go by our feelings. We have to ask God to help us to forgive. We might have to pray and fast to let go of some forgiveness. But if you want God's blessing to be in your life, you have to do whatever it takes to forgive. When we don't forgive someone who hurts us, we put our trust in them and not God. However, when we put our trust in God, we will forgive them over and over again. So be determined that people will not stop your blessings.

We should do the same thing for people that God does for us. He keeps on forgiving us no matter how many times we mess up. The Lord has already told us that love thinks no evil. You have to love them and forgive, but you don't have to let them be a best friend. I have to forgive you, but I don't have to let you make my life miserable. Ask the Lord to tell you how to handle those tough situations, especially those personal relationships with someone that you see on a regular base that might hurt you. The Bible tells us that the measure we use will be measured back to us.

I asked the Lord why I have to always be the first one to do what is right. The Holy Spirit told me that the glory I am getting ready to walk you in to is all worth it. He explained to me the more I walk in perfect love and do what is right and don't fight my battle but let the Lord do it for me, He will answer my prays and gives me my heart desire. God blesses you so you can bless someone else. One way to keep God's blessing in your life is to bless others. I am not always talking about giving them money. I am talking about encouraging someone and lifting up a hurting person with your faith in God.

When you love and put your whole heart into it do not worry about getting hurt, just put your trust in God. By the end of the relationship, you will have no regrets because you put your faith in God. Even if something happens, you will not have to say that I should have done things differently. You will have no regrets. If you have to say, "I am sorry. Please forgive me" it frees you. You have to give an account of what you do. Miserable people make other people miserable. Your words can be very powerful. You should not use your words negatively. It is like putting a gun to someone's head and pulling the trigger.

Godly parents and spouses do not use negative words. Do not destroy the people God gave you to take care of. Stop taking your anger out on the people that will be there for you when everyone else is gone. Hug your love ones daily and let them know you love them. We hug friends more than we hug our love ones. I asked God to help me to use my words to encourage not to hurt people. Matthew 12: 36 says, that "every idle word that men shall speak, they shall give an account thereof in the day of judgement."

The Lord assures us in this battle of life that we don't have to fight. The Lord will give you what to do. Remember what God's Word says will stand forever. When someone says something negative to you, don't let it affect you. This is just the enemy trying to lower your self-esteem. Negative people have low self-esteem. They are trying to make you miserable like them. Avoid negative people and pray about how to talk to them. Quote scripture or sing a song. The Lord has already told you that revenge is His. We already know that we will give an account for every idol word that comes out of our mouths. We have to teach our children not to use negative words, too. God commands us to forgive and to walk in perfect love. We have to forgive when we don't want to forgive. We must walk in perfect love or we will stop our blessing. God has forgiven us so why can't we forgive someone else.

The Bible tells us that love thinks no evil. You will stop God's blessing from your life when you take offense when people do you wrong. It also stops your blessings when you don't forgive. Be willing to say I'm sorry even when it is not your fault and, especially, if you have hurt someone else's feeling. When forgiving gets hard, you have to ask the Lord to help you. Not forgiving will cut your blessings out of your life. When someone offends you, do not hold it in, simply ask the Lord to help you to deal with it in a positive way. When you hold offense, you are allowing that person to stop your blessing. Roman 8:31 says, "What shall we say then to these things? If God be for us who can be against us?" When people try to stop you from something God has for you, push that much harder and do not give up. Even when doors close, God will sometimes open a window. So do not give up until the Holy Spirit says, "It is enough." If that doesn't work know that if you trust God through it, He has something else better for you. God will give you double for your trouble.

After going through a struggle with people trying to offend me on every side, I learned God's faithfulness. Out of this struggle came some of my greatest blessings. All I had to do was trust God and keep the faith. Isaiah 54:17 says that no weapon that is formed against me shall prosper, and every tongue that rise against me in judgment that God shall condemn.

Obedience is one of the most important things we can be. We have to be obedient to whatever the Lord tell us to do. When we listen to the instruction of God, He blesses us the more. Problems don't last that long and because we are in the will of God, we will make it through. The Lord our God told us to acknowledge Him in all our ways and He shall direct our way. Obedience is better than sacrifice. Always be obedient to the Lord and be a blessing to others. If you don't know how, let the Lord show and tell you how. When we let God handle our problems and learn how to bless someone else, we are being obedient to the Word of God. This is a sign that your life is moving to a better state. When you acknowledge God and be obedient to what God tells you, then you can say "no weapon that is formed against me shall prosper." It may form but it shall not prosper. Be obedient to what God and His Word tells you to do.

When you put fear under your feet, your end result will always be victorious. When the devil attacks someone you love, this can be

the hardest fear to control. Trusting and obeying God is the most important step in this faith walk. If you want peace in your life, let faith in God defeat all fear. Use God's Word to conquer fear. Don't just say the first scripture you learned as a child, declare scripture that pertains to that problem. God will perfect those things which concerns you. Do as I have done… Choose to stand on the Word of God when your fear comes.

My son Joshua was a sophomore in high school and his grades were not necessarily Clemson material. This is when God started working on Joshua's behalf. Joshua started improving his grades, and he graduated from high school with honors. When it was time to apply to colleges, Joshua sent applications to different colleges, including Clemson, but was not sure of what college would accept him. He brought acceptance letters from other colleges for me to sign, but not only was I lead not to sign them, I was instructed to tear them up and throw them away. I had to be obedient to God, no matter how things looked. Joshua did not realize that God spoke to me and told me that he was going to Clemson. While this may sound normal, you must know that my son felt he would not be accepted to Clemson. It was getting close to starting college and Joshua came to me and asked, "Mom are you sure God said that I was going to Clemson? You know I didn't get an acceptance letter yet?"

While everyone doubted that Joshua was going to go to Clemson, I trusted God in the midst of doubt and fear. The very next day, his acceptance letter from Clemson came in the mail. That's when Joshua and I started praising God. This was our proof that God is faithful and if we obey Him, he will indeed bless us. I am determined to continue to be faithful to Him, because of His faithfulness towards me. AMEN!

CHAPTER FOUR

Create

It's important to create your own destiny by learning to trust and rest in God. This simply means that you will gain confidence in Jesus, knowing that he will take care of what concerns you. We don't have to fix things ourselves. Jesus loves us enough to fix it for us. As we learn to rest and ask the Lord how to handle oppositions when they occur, we understand that all things will work together for our good. When we walk in perfect love, we can rest without fear, because perfect love brings God on the scene, knowing that He will fight our battle. When you stop fighting people and let God do the fighting, you become free to create the environment that will fertilize your calling. You have to ask God to teach you how to rest in Him so you can create your own destiny.

I made my decision to rest in the Lord, having all confidence that God would fix my situation just right for me. And He did. I have found no better feeling than resting in God. The more I learn how to rest, the freer I become. When I have a problem, I take it to God and leave it there. Then, when I pick up my problem, I ask God to forgive me for not believing that he could handle it. I repeat His Word, "I shall walk and not faint." I remind myself, "Wait on the Lord and be of good courage." It has been tested and proven that whenever I try to fix things for God (just like Sarah did), I mess things up and make the reality of my destiny that much longer.

One way you can rest in God is to obey His Word. Proverbs 3:6 says, "In all thy ways acknowledge him and he shall direct thy path." When things go wrong and you acknowledge God, you can stand still. God will honor His Word; He will fix it for you. You can rest in the Word of God. Thus, to rest in God you have to know the Word of God. So when the enemy comes in you can speak the Word out loud. One of my favorite scriptures is Psalm 138:8, which reminds me to never be in despair no matter how great the torment; if I cry to God with trust in Him He will deliver me. When I quote scriptures like, "The LORD will perfect that which concerneth me: thy mercy, O LORD, endureth forever: forsake not the works of thine own hands," I believe that nothing will happen to me that will not bring me to a perfect end. The Bible states in Jeremiah 29:11, "For I know the thoughts that I think toward you said the Lord, thoughts of peace and not of evil to give you an expected end."

If someone gets upset with you, don't give place to the devil and fight them back. Let the Lord fight the situation for you. If you try to fight every battle you will be miserable. Even the simple battles, just let the Lord fight them for you. You will see how rested and at peace you will feel. The Word says, "You will reap what you sow." Let the Lord take revenge for you. You don't want to be going through something all your life; being sad and depressed because of things you did to yourself and others. When you stop fighting and start resting in God, your destiny will take its place.

Truly, when God gets ready to bless you, situations arise that makes you want to fight back. Instead of letting go and letting God, you retaliate and hold up your blessings. As you release your will, you will start to soar like an eagle. Then, your destiny will be as God has called it to be. Don't start pecking like the chicken, grabbing this and that. You will not let negative people hinder you and when the devil sees he cannot stop you from reaching your destiny, he will have to back up and leave you.

Trust our Father God and He will give you the fuel you need to become more obedient to God and become a better Christian. When you keep the faith and do not waver, whatever the enemy tries God will turn it around for your good. So rest in the Lord and keep the right frame of mind about everything. As your body and mind become stressed, God will turn things around and you will become blessed. Don't speak negative and watch God work things out for you. Even when the devil turns up the heat, you continue to rest in God. Remember that the enemy's days are numbered and your life has purpose.

If you be about God's work when things are not going your way and when you don't' feel like doing, God will start to turn things around in your heart first and then in your situation. As you finish fasting and praying, the devil will come and fight you the more, just like he did with Jesus. But don't back up. Don't give in. Just know that the greater the struggle, the better the blessing. Keep trusting and believing.

That's why trusting God is one of the most vital things we have to do when we can't see God in our situation. If we trust God during that time, everything will be alright. We have to make a decision to trust Him. When the pain gets greater than we can bear, if we trust God he will turn our mourning into dancing. We serve an incredible God that can and will turn anything around. The harder the devil fights you, fight even harder to live right and do what is right. I promise you God will start blessing your life.

It's not that the enemy is going to stop trying to stop, block, and hinder you, but he will never be successful. Remember, if you continue to trust God, you will find that there is no failure in God. It may not go as you plan, but you still trust God and it will always end up great. Stop trying to be accepted by people and learn to be accepted by God. While people will always let you down, God will never let you down. The only thing you owe man is love and respect.

The Bible tells us to put our trust in God and not man. You have to believe that there is no mountain high enough, no valley low enough, no river wide enough to keep God from rescuing you. There is no pain God can't heal, no sorrow he can't end and no enemy that he can't stop. When the enemy comes in and tells you anything different from the Word of God, stand therefore with your loins gird about with truth, knowing that your trust and dependence is in the Word of God. It is the Word that gives us just what we need to help us in our times of need. All we have to do is ask him to help us and He will.

Ask the Lord to help you be a better person. Little by little you will see your life getting better and better. As we trust and rest in God's Word despite the bad things that get us down, we will see a change in our attitude and condition. No matter what comes your way, rest and trust in God and He will cause you to rise out of your dilemma. The Lord will be the lifter of your head while you are going through. It is when we go through the fire of our tests and trials that God will burn off so much unnecessary baggage and give us a more forgiving heart. We won't be concerned about other people's business, but will be concerned about their souls. We will stop gossiping about the sisters and brothers and will start praying for them. Even when they try to destroy you, let God worry about that for you. Philippians 4: 7 says, "And the peace of God, which passeth all understanding, shall keep your hearts and minds through Christ Jesus."

My Testimony

Sometimes your five senses will tell you that you are not going to survive the test or trial. It may seem that the things you are going through will never end. No matter how hard you pray, you can sense when the devil start messing. You can't put your hand on it, but it doesn't feel good, it doesn't taste good, it doesn't smell good, and surely doesn't look good. Everything around you is telling you that you are not going to survive. You even get a bitter taste in your mouth from your experiences. Do as I have done… Create your own destiny by trusting the Word of God.

From a child my only daughter, Brittney was always precise, neat, and calculated what she wanted to do. Brittney is a good student, but she had doubts whether she could get her chemistry degree after her sophomore year. Chemistry was her desired major but she felt discouraged because she was not doing as well as she had hoped. When she started taking chemistry courses, classes started getting harder and she wanted to change her major. Even her professor told her that he hated parents who tell their children they could do all things through Jesus; implying that it would take natural intelligence to accomplish any goal and not God giving the knowledge to make it happen. I brought my children up to love God and know that He provides them with the power, smarts, and ability to do all things. Even when things get hard, God can help you out of your situation. Brittney did not feel she was going to graduate from Lander College with her chemistry degree. However, through faith in our unchanging God, I told her not to give up, but pray and fast so that God would answer our prayers. I also told her that God is not going to give her a dream and not give her the ability to make it come true. Getting a chemistry degree was her dream and she and our entire family started to fast and pray on her behalf. Instead of giving up, Brittney renewed her strength and God gave her what she needed to do well in the rest of her classes. Our family once again witnessed God's faithfulness when Brittney graduated with her chemistry degree from Lander College. She is now working in her field and praying for direction to go to another level. Brittney is now walking in her destiny. Praise the Lord.

There is a song that says, **I've learned how to live Holy, I've learned how to live right, I've learned how to suffer, cause if I suffer, I will gain eternal life**.

I learned to trust God and His Word enough to keep on dancing through the pain and hurt. Then, I watched God change things for me. I relied on the Word and came out alright every time. Roman 8:28 says, "And we know that all things work together for good to those who love God to those who are called according to his purpose." I believe that the Lord loves me and all things will work out for my good. AMEN!

CHAPTER FIVE

What's Your Testimony?

Why is my testimony successful? I just learned to use the 4 C's on my sojourn here. You can too! In every situation, remember to **confess** your sins, **claim** your righteousness and that you will live for Him, **choose** to stay focused on God's purpose for your life, **create** your own destiny by trusting God to fight your battles.

Keep a journal of these 4 C's and share your testimony with others too.

It's your turn to tell your testimony.
We all have to make the decision for ourselves.
Do you want a successful testimony or a defeated one?

All you have to do is
Confess, Claim, Choose, and Create!

My Name is

_____
and I want to share my testimony.

THE 4 C's OF A SUCCESSFUL TESTIMONY

I Confess *my sins, what I want God to do, and that I am helpless without God.*

This is my testimony:

_____

_____

_____

_____

_____

_____

_____

_____

_____

_____

AMEN!

RUBINA ROBERTS

I Claim that I am a follower of Jesus and that I will live for Him.

This is my testimony:

_____

_____

_____

_____

_____

_____

_____

_____

_____

_____

AMEN!

THE 4 C's OF A SUCCESSFUL TESTIMONY

I Choose to stay focused on God's purpose for my life, to forgive others, and to be obedient to God.

This is my testimony:

_____

_____

_____

_____

_____

_____

_____

_____

_____

_____

AMEN!

I Create my own destiny by trusting
God to fight my battles.

This is my testimony:

_____

_____

_____

_____

_____

_____

_____

_____

_____

_____

AMEN!

ABOUT THE AUTHOR

Rubina Roberts is striving to be a virtuous woman. She is married with four children and they reside in Walterboro, South Carolina. Rubina's main goal is blessing others, because she has learned that the more you bless others, the more God will bless you. Rubina Roberts loves to praise the Lord for all His goodness.

www.ingramcontent.com/pod-product-compliance
Lightning Source LLC
LaVergne TN
LVHW051712080426
835511LV00017B/2878